It's A Different Story

It's A Different Healing

Set In Soul

© 2018 Tatiana Media LLC in partnership with Set In Soul LLC

ISBN #: 978-1-7321075-9-5

Published by Tatiana Media LLC

All rights reserved. No part of this journal/publication may be reproduced, stored in a retrieval system, or transmitted in any form or by any means, electronic, mechanical, photocopying, recording, scanning, or otherwise, except as permitted under Section 107 or 108 of the 1976 United States Copyright Act whatsoever without express written permission from the author, except in the case of brief quotations embodied in critical articles and reviews. Please refer all pertinent questions to the publisher.

Limit of Liability/Disclaimer of Warranty: While the publisher and author have used their best efforts in preparing this book/journal, they make no representations or warranties with respect to the accuracy or completeness of the contents of this book/journal and specifically disclaim any implied warranties. The advice and strategies contained herein may not be suitable for your situation. You should consult with a professional where appropriate. Neither the publisher nor author shall be liable for any loss of profit or any other emotional, physical, spiritual and mental distress and damages, including but not limited to special, incidental, consequential, or other damages.

For general information on our other products and services, please contact our Customer Support within the United States at support@setinsoul.com.

Tatiana Media LLC as well as Set In Soul LLC publishes its books in a variety of electronic formats. Some content that appears in print may not be available in electronic books.

This Journal Belongs To

_____

Dedicated To A Love I Will Never Leave Behind. You Will Always Be With Me.

Table Of Contents

How To Use This Journal	6
Saying Goodbye	7
Healing From Heartbreak	10
Peacefully Moving Forward	23

How To Use This Journal

There are so many misconceptions about miscarrying, but one of the biggest ones is thinking that it is your fault. It is NOT your fault. As excited as you were to prepare for your baby to come into this world, God had a better plan. We know that this is not easy to hear or even what you want to read, but it is the truth. This may be a difficult time for you trying to figure out the why, and just mourning the loss of your baby. This journal is here to help you get through your loss. The pain may never go away, but there is a way to move forward with a mindset and spirit of happiness, gratitude, and excitement for what is to come. Your prayers will be answered. Your prayers are always answered. We believe this. But to move towards this direction of thinking, there must be an acknowledgment that healing needs to take place. That healing encompasses being able to forgive yourself and others for what happened. Healing in this regard means that you must have faith that what you desire in your heart is aligned with God's word and will manifest in your life. When you use this journal, you are facing yourself and allowing yourself to go through the process of healing from what was inside of you. This is you facing you as well as you being a best friend to yourself. You can express your hurt, anger, frustrations, and pain here and through time you will be able to feel and notice a healing within your mind, body, and spirit. A miscarriage doesn't happen to you to hurt you but to make you stronger. It is an event that is set up so you can increase your faith. While you may feel no one understands how you're feeling or your partner may not communicate how he feels, this is your space to be able to let it all out. You are never alone in your journey. God is with you. You have this journal because it is time to move forward.

We recommend using this journal daily. Fill out the daily prompts every morning to set the tone for your day and reconfigure your mind. The daily prompts are repetitive on purpose. It is through this way you can track your growth. The first section of this journal called 'Saying Goodbye' sets the tone for this journal. This is where you will speak directly to your baby about the things you wanted them to know. Our daily prompts are designed to build you up and increase your faith as well as make you stronger. This journal has motivational prompts sprinkled throughout this journal as well as freestyling sections where you can simply express your thoughts. This is your space. These are your words. You deserve this. It's time to heal.

Saying Goodbye

Saying Goodbye

Name Your Child:

Give Your Child A Conceive Date (Estimate):

Tell Your Child What You Want Them To Know About You:

Tell Your Child Why Your Heart Is/Was Empty:

Tell Your Child What You Think They Know About You:

Saying Goodbye

What Do You Want Your Child To Know In General?

Write A Prayer For Your Child:

Write A Prayer For Your Healing Heart:

Tell Your Child Why You Are Grateful To Them:

Tell Your Child Why Your Heart Is Now Full:

Healing From Heartbreak

Healing From Heartbreak

I've Experienced My First Miscarriage At The Age Of:

I Have Experienced (Write Down How Many Miscarriages):

How Far Was I When I Miscarried?

I Knew I Miscarried When:

During The Pregnancy, I Felt:

Healing From Heartbreak

My Miscarriage Has Taught Me:

Miscarrying Made Me Feel:

I Don't Understand:

I Do Understand:

It's Been Hard For Me:

Healing From Heartbreak

Do I Cry?

If Yes To The Prompt Above, Why To The Tears?

My Partner Feels:

We Were Expecting:

We Wanted:

Healing From Heartbreak

My Partner Wanted:

I Wanted:

My Baby Was Suppose To Be:

I'm Not Sure That:

I Had No Idea:

Healing From Heartbreak

I Feel:

My Support System During This Time:

I Have Chosen:

Who Do I Blame For The Miscarriage?

Why Do I Believe I Miscarried?

Healing From Heartbreak

I Broke The News That I Miscarried To:

When (Regarding The Prompt Above)?

I Feel Guilty About (Answer If Applicable):

Other Women In My Family Who Have Experienced A Miscarriage: (Answer If Applicable):

I Am Angry Because:

Healing From Heartbreak

It's Okay For Me Not To:

When I See Other Pregnant Women, I Feel:

Everyone Expects Me To Feel:

Things People Say That I Don't Like To Hear:

I Believe Miscarriage Is:

Healing From Heartbreak

Miscarriage Doesn't Define:

I Hold On To:

I Am Accepting:

During This Time, I Am Being Gentle With Myself By:

Do I Want To Try To Conceive Again?

Healing From Heartbreak

I Believe My Body:

I Was Just Beginning To:

I Know I Can:

My Heart, Mind, And Spirit Are Open To:

My Heart, Mind, And Spirit Are Closed To:

Healing From Heartbreak

I'm In A Space Where:

Right Now I Desire:

I Believe:

What I Believe About Myself:

I Am Capable Of:

Healing From Heartbreak

I Am Strong Enough To:

I Am Ready To:

Some Days I Feel:

Other Days I Feel:

I Never Had Time To Feel:

Healing From Heartbreak

I Now Have A Desire To:

I Have Made Peace With:

How Did I Say Goodbye?

My Outlook On Life Now:

My Future Approach To My Upcoming Pregnancies (Answer If Applicable):

Peacefully Moving Forward

Peacefully Moving Forward

Date: Mood:

Today's Affirmation: I Am Learning:

I Am Intentionally Deciding: Today I Will Silence My Inner Critic By:

I Am Releasing: Today's Prayer:

Today I Have Hope That: I Look Forward To:

Today's Self Love Activity: My Promise To Myself:

My Thoughts

Peacefully Moving Forward

Date: Mood:

Today's Affirmation: I Am Learning:

I Am Intentionally Deciding: Today I Will Silence My Inner Critic By:

I Am Releasing: Today's Prayer:

Today I Have Hope That: I Look Forward To:

Today's Self Love Activity: My Promise To Myself:

My Thoughts

You Will Always Be My Angel.

God Needed You Back.

Peacefully Moving Forward

Date: Mood:

Today's Affirmation: I Am Learning:

I Am Intentionally Deciding: Today I Will Silence My Inner Critic By:

I Am Releasing: Today's Prayer:

Today I Have Hope That: I Look Forward To:

Today's Self Love Activity: My Promise To Myself:

My Thoughts

Peacefully Moving Forward

Date: Mood:

Today's Affirmation: I Am Learning:

I Am Intentionally Deciding: Today I Will Silence My Inner Critic By:

I Am Releasing: Today's Prayer:

Today I Have Hope That: I Look Forward To:

Today's Self Love Activity: My Promise To Myself:

My Thoughts

A List Of All The Reasons Why I Loved You....

Dear God, Take Care Of My Baby Please.

Peacefully Moving Forward

Date: Mood:

Today's Affirmation: I Am Learning:

I Am Intentionally Deciding: Today I Will Silence My Inner Critic By:

I Am Releasing: Today's Prayer:

Today I Have Hope That: I Look Forward To:

Today's Self Love Activity: My Promise To Myself:

My Thoughts

Peacefully Moving Forward

Date: Mood:

Today's Affirmation: I Am Learning:

I Am Intentionally Deciding: Today I Will Silence My Inner Critic By:

I Am Releasing: Today's Prayer:

Today I Have Hope That: I Look Forward To:

Today's Self Love Activity: My Promise To Myself:

My Thoughts

Why Do I Feel So Sad?

I Miss You.

Peacefully Moving Forward

Date: Mood:

Today's Affirmation: I Am Learning:

I Am Intentionally Deciding: Today I Will Silence My Inner Critic By:

I Am Releasing: Today's Prayer:

Today I Have Hope That: I Look Forward To:

Today's Self Love Activity: My Promise To Myself:

My Thoughts

Peacefully Moving Forward

Date: Mood:

Today's Affirmation: I Am Learning:

I Am Intentionally Deciding: Today I Will Silence My Inner Critic By:

I Am Releasing: Today's Prayer:

Today I Have Hope That: I Look Forward To:

Today's Self Love Activity: My Promise To Myself:

My Thoughts

Am I Ready To Try Again?

You Were In Me To Show Me It Is Possible.

Peacefully Moving Forward

Date: Mood:

Today's Affirmation: I Am Learning:

I Am Intentionally Deciding: Today I Will Silence My Inner Critic By:

I Am Releasing: Today's Prayer:

Today I Have Hope That: I Look Forward To:

Today's Self Love Activity: My Promise To Myself:

My Thoughts

Peacefully Moving Forward

Date: Mood:

Today's Affirmation: I Am Learning:

I Am Intentionally Deciding: Today I Will Silence My Inner Critic By:

I Am Releasing: Today's Prayer:

Today I Have Hope That: I Look Forward To:

Today's Self Love Activity: My Promise To Myself:

My Thoughts

Peacefully Moving Forward

Date: Mood:

Today's Affirmation: I Am Learning:

I Am Intentionally Deciding: Today I Will Silence My Inner Critic By:

I Am Releasing: Today's Prayer:

Today I Have Hope That: I Look Forward To:

Today's Self Love Activity: My Promise To Myself:

My Thoughts

Peacefully Moving Forward

Date: Mood:

Today's Affirmation: I Am Learning:

I Am Intentionally Deciding: Today I Will Silence My Inner Critic By:

I Am Releasing: Today's Prayer:

Today I Have Hope That: I Look Forward To:

Today's Self Love Activity: My Promise To Myself:

My Thoughts

I'm Happy To Know That As Long As You Were With Me, The Only Thing You Felt Was Love.

Your Heart Will Always Be A Part Of Mine.

Peacefully Moving Forward

Date: Mood:

Today's Affirmation: I Am Learning:

I Am Intentionally Deciding: Today I Will Silence My Inner Critic By:

I Am Releasing: Today's Prayer:

Today I Have Hope That: I Look Forward To:

Today's Self Love Activity: My Promise To Myself:

My Thoughts

Peacefully Moving Forward

Date: Mood:

Today's Affirmation: I Am Learning:

I Am Intentionally Deciding: Today I Will Silence My Inner Critic By:

I Am Releasing: Today's Prayer:

Today I Have Hope That: I Look Forward To:

Today's Self Love Activity: My Promise To Myself:

My Thoughts

Peacefully Moving Forward

Date: Mood:

Today's Affirmation: I Am Learning:

I Am Intentionally Deciding: Today I Will Silence My Inner Critic By:

I Am Releasing: Today's Prayer:

Today I Have Hope That: I Look Forward To:

Today's Self Love Activity: My Promise To Myself:

My Thoughts

Peacefully Moving Forward

Date: Mood:

Today's Affirmation: I Am Learning:

I Am Intentionally Deciding: Today I Will Silence My Inner Critic By:

I Am Releasing: Today's Prayer:

Today I Have Hope That: I Look Forward To:

Today's Self Love Activity: My Promise To Myself:

My Thoughts

Peacefully Moving Forward

Date: Mood:

Today's Affirmation: I Am Learning:

I Am Intentionally Deciding: Today I Will Silence My Inner Critic By:

I Am Releasing: Today's Prayer:

Today I Have Hope That: I Look Forward To:

Today's Self Love Activity: My Promise To Myself:

My Thoughts

My Partner And I Are Helping Each Other To Heal By....

When I Think Of You, I Just Think Of The Love You Gave Me.

Peacefully Moving Forward

Date: Mood:

Today's Affirmation: I Am Learning:

I Am Intentionally Deciding: Today I Will Silence My Inner Critic By:

I Am Releasing: Today's Prayer:

Today I Have Hope That: I Look Forward To:

Today's Self Love Activity: My Promise To Myself:

My Thoughts

Peacefully Moving Forward

Date: Mood:

Today's Affirmation: I Am Learning:

I Am Intentionally Deciding: Today I Will Silence My Inner Critic By:

I Am Releasing: Today's Prayer:

Today I Have Hope That: I Look Forward To:

Today's Self Love Activity: My Promise To Myself:

My Thoughts

Peacefully Moving Forward

Date: Mood:

Today's Affirmation: I Am Learning:

I Am Intentionally Deciding: Today I Will Silence My Inner Critic By:

I Am Releasing: Today's Prayer:

Today I Have Hope That: I Look Forward To:

Today's Self Love Activity: My Promise To Myself:

My Thoughts

I Know My Baby....

A Moment In My Belly But A Lifetime In My Heart.

Peacefully Moving Forward

Date: Mood:

Today's Affirmation: I Am Learning:

I Am Intentionally Deciding: Today I Will Silence My Inner Critic By:

I Am Releasing: Today's Prayer:

Today I Have Hope That: I Look Forward To:

Today's Self Love Activity: My Promise To Myself:

My Thoughts

Peacefully Moving Forward

Date: Mood:

Today's Affirmation: I Am Learning:

I Am Intentionally Deciding: Today I Will Silence My Inner Critic By:

I Am Releasing: Today's Prayer:

Today I Have Hope That: I Look Forward To:

Today's Self Love Activity: My Promise To Myself:

My Thoughts

I'm Blessed That You Decided To Come And Live Within Me Before Going To Heaven.

You Were Too Special To Be Here.

Peacefully Moving Forward

Date: Mood:

Today's Affirmation: I Am Learning:

I Am Intentionally Deciding: Today I Will Silence My Inner Critic By:

I Am Releasing: Today's Prayer:

Today I Have Hope That: I Look Forward To:

Today's Self Love Activity: My Promise To Myself:

My Thoughts

Peacefully Moving Forward

Date: Mood:

Today's Affirmation: | I Am Learning:

I Am Intentionally Deciding: | Today I Will Silence My Inner Critic By:

I Am Releasing: | Today's Prayer:

Today I Have Hope That: | I Look Forward To:

Today's Self Love Activity: | My Promise To Myself:

My Thoughts

I Know You Are Calling Me Mommy From Heaven And I Hear You.

My Time With You Will Be One I Will Never Forget.

Peacefully Moving Forward

Date: Mood:

Today's Affirmation: I Am Learning:

I Am Intentionally Deciding: Today I Will Silence My Inner Critic By:

I Am Releasing: Today's Prayer:

Today I Have Hope That: I Look Forward To:

Today's Self Love Activity: My Promise To Myself:

My Thoughts

Peacefully Moving Forward

Date: Mood:

Today's Affirmation: I Am Learning:

I Am Intentionally Deciding: Today I Will Silence My Inner Critic By:

I Am Releasing: Today's Prayer:

Today I Have Hope That: I Look Forward To:

Today's Self Love Activity: My Promise To Myself:

My Thoughts

I Will Be The Mommy You Want Me To Be.

It Hurts Because I Loved You. I Prayed For You.

Peacefully Moving Forward

Date: Mood:

Today's Affirmation: I Am Learning:

I Am Intentionally Deciding: Today I Will Silence My Inner Critic By:

I Am Releasing: Today's Prayer:

Today I Have Hope That: I Look Forward To:

Today's Self Love Activity: My Promise To Myself:

My Thoughts

Peacefully Moving Forward

Date: Mood:

Today's Affirmation: I Am Learning:

I Am Intentionally Deciding: Today I Will Silence My Inner Critic By:

I Am Releasing: Today's Prayer:

Today I Have Hope That: I Look Forward To:

Today's Self Love Activity: My Promise To Myself:

My Thoughts

I Am Getting Better At....

But The Lord Stood By Me And Strengthened Me

2 Timothey 4:17

Peacefully Moving Forward

Date: Mood:

Today's Affirmation: I Am Learning:

I Am Intentionally Deciding: Today I Will Silence My Inner Critic By:

I Am Releasing: Today's Prayer:

Today I Have Hope That: I Look Forward To:

Today's Self Love Activity: My Promise To Myself:

My Thoughts

Peacefully Moving Forward

Date: Mood:

Today's Affirmation: I Am Learning:

I Am Intentionally Deciding: Today I Will Silence My Inner Critic By:

I Am Releasing: Today's Prayer:

Today I Have Hope That: I Look Forward To:

Today's Self Love Activity: My Promise To Myself:

My Thoughts

Peacefully Moving Forward

Date: Mood:

Today's Affirmation: I Am Learning:

I Am Intentionally Deciding: Today I Will Silence My Inner Critic By:

I Am Releasing: Today's Prayer:

Today I Have Hope That: I Look Forward To:

Today's Self Love Activity: My Promise To Myself:

My Thoughts

The Best Way For Me To Heal And Move Forward....

Love Me Through The Pain Of Losing You.

Peacefully Moving Forward

Date: Mood:

Today's Affirmation: I Am Learning:

I Am Intentionally Deciding: Today I Will Silence My Inner Critic By:

I Am Releasing: Today's Prayer:

Today I Have Hope That: I Look Forward To:

Today's Self Love Activity: My Promise To Myself:

My Thoughts

Peacefully Moving Forward

Date: Mood:

Today's Affirmation: I Am Learning:

I Am Intentionally Deciding: Today I Will Silence My Inner Critic By:

I Am Releasing: Today's Prayer:

Today I Have Hope That: I Look Forward To:

Today's Self Love Activity: My Promise To Myself:

My Thoughts

I Know You Are Saying Give It One More Try.

I
Am
Sorry.

Peacefully Moving Forward

Date: Mood:

Today's Affirmation: I Am Learning:

I Am Intentionally Deciding: Today I Will Silence My Inner Critic By:

I Am Releasing: Today's Prayer:

Today I Have Hope That: I Look Forward To:

Today's Self Love Activity: My Promise To Myself:

My Thoughts

Peacefully Moving Forward

Date: Mood:

Today's Affirmation: I Am Learning:

I Am Intentionally Deciding: Today I Will Silence My Inner Critic By:

I Am Releasing: Today's Prayer:

Today I Have Hope That: I Look Forward To:

Today's Self Love Activity: My Promise To Myself:

My Thoughts

I'm Okay With You Watching Over Me.

I Will Always Be Your Mother.

Peacefully Moving Forward

Date: Mood:

Today's Affirmation: I Am Learning:

I Am Intentionally Deciding: Today I Will Silence My Inner Critic By:

I Am Releasing: Today's Prayer:

Today I Have Hope That: I Look Forward To:

Today's Self Love Activity: My Promise To Myself:

My Thoughts

Peacefully Moving Forward

Date: Mood:

Today's Affirmation: | I Am Learning:

I Am Intentionally Deciding: | Today I Will Silence My Inner Critic By:

I Am Releasing: | Today's Prayer:

Today I Have Hope That: | I Look Forward To:

Today's Self Love Activity: | My Promise To Myself:

My Thoughts

Peacefully Moving Forward

Date: Mood:

Today's Affirmation: I Am Learning:

I Am Intentionally Deciding: Today I Will Silence My Inner Critic By:

I Am Releasing: Today's Prayer:

Today I Have Hope That: I Look Forward To:

Today's Self Love Activity: My Promise To Myself:

My Thoughts

You Have Changed My Life For The Better.

I Will Always Speak Life Upon You.

Peacefully Moving Forward

Date: Mood:

Today's Affirmation: I Am Learning:

I Am Intentionally Deciding: Today I Will Silence My Inner Critic By:

I Am Releasing: Today's Prayer:

Today I Have Hope That: I Look Forward To:

Today's Self Love Activity: My Promise To Myself:

My Thoughts

Peacefully Moving Forward

Date: Mood:

Today's Affirmation: I Am Learning:

I Am Intentionally Deciding: Today I Will Silence My Inner Critic By:

I Am Releasing: Today's Prayer:

Today I Have Hope That: I Look Forward To:

Today's Self Love Activity: My Promise To Myself:

My Thoughts

Peacefully Moving Forward

Date: Mood:

Today's Affirmation: I Am Learning:

I Am Intentionally Deciding: Today I Will Silence My Inner Critic By:

I Am Releasing: Today's Prayer:

Today I Have Hope That: I Look Forward To:

Today's Self Love Activity: My Promise To Myself:

My Thoughts

I Would Tell Other Women Who Miscarried....

Strength For Today. Hope For Tomorrow.

Peacefully Moving Forward

Date: Mood:

Today's Affirmation: I Am Learning:

I Am Intentionally Deciding: Today I Will Silence My Inner Critic By:

I Am Releasing: Today's Prayer:

Today I Have Hope That: I Look Forward To:

Today's Self Love Activity: My Promise To Myself:

My Thoughts

Peacefully Moving Forward

Date: Mood:

Today's Affirmation: I Am Learning:

I Am Intentionally Deciding: Today I Will Silence My Inner Critic By:

I Am Releasing: Today's Prayer:

Today I Have Hope That: I Look Forward To:

Today's Self Love Activity: My Promise To Myself:

My Thoughts

I Know Your Story Will Continue With Me.

There Is Good In Every Situation.

Peacefully Moving Forward

Date: Mood:

Today's Affirmation: I Am Learning:

I Am Intentionally Deciding: Today I Will Silence My Inner Critic By:

I Am Releasing: Today's Prayer:

Today I Have Hope That: I Look Forward To:

Today's Self Love Activity: My Promise To Myself:

My Thoughts

I Am Lifting Myself Up Through This Pain.

This Isn't The End. Not For You. Not For Me. Not For Us.

Peacefully Moving Forward

Date: Mood:

Today's Affirmation: I Am Learning:

I Am Intentionally Deciding: Today I Will Silence My Inner Critic By:

I Am Releasing: Today's Prayer:

Today I Have Hope That: I Look Forward To:

Today's Self Love Activity: My Promise To Myself:

My Thoughts

Peacefully Moving Forward

Date: Mood:

Today's Affirmation: I Am Learning:

I Am Intentionally Deciding: Today I Will Silence My Inner Critic By:

I Am Releasing: Today's Prayer:

Today I Have Hope That: I Look Forward To:

Today's Self Love Activity: My Promise To Myself:

My Thoughts

I Have Learned....

One Day Closer To A Stronger Me.

Peacefully Moving Forward

Date: Mood:

Today's Affirmation: I Am Learning:

I Am Intentionally Deciding: Today I Will Silence My Inner Critic By:

I Am Releasing: Today's Prayer:

Today I Have Hope That: I Look Forward To:

Today's Self Love Activity: My Promise To Myself:

My Thoughts

Peacefully Moving Forward

Date: Mood:

Today's Affirmation: I Am Learning:

I Am Intentionally Deciding: Today I Will Silence My Inner Critic By:

I Am Releasing: Today's Prayer:

Today I Have Hope That: I Look Forward To:

Today's Self Love Activity: My Promise To Myself:

My Thoughts

I Find Happiness In....

I Will Not Worry About What Happens Next.

Peacefully Moving Forward

Date: Mood:

Today's Affirmation: I Am Learning:

I Am Intentionally Deciding: Today I Will Silence My Inner Critic By:

I Am Releasing: Today's Prayer:

Today I Have Hope That: I Look Forward To:

Today's Self Love Activity: My Promise To Myself:

My Thoughts

Peacefully Moving Forward

Date: Mood:

Today's Affirmation: I Am Learning:

I Am Intentionally Deciding: Today I Will Silence My Inner Critic By:

I Am Releasing: Today's Prayer:

Today I Have Hope That: I Look Forward To:

Today's Self Love Activity: My Promise To Myself:

My Thoughts

I Still Trust In God. I Believe In What He Says About Me.

At The End Of The Night, The Sun Always Shines.

Peacefully Moving Forward

Date: Mood:

Today's Affirmation: I Am Learning:

I Am Intentionally Deciding: Today I Will Silence My Inner Critic By:

I Am Releasing: Today's Prayer:

Today I Have Hope That: I Look Forward To:

Today's Self Love Activity: My Promise To Myself:

My Thoughts

Peacefully Moving Forward

Date: Mood:

Today's Affirmation: I Am Learning:

I Am Intentionally Deciding: Today I Will Silence My Inner Critic By:

I Am Releasing: Today's Prayer:

Today I Have Hope That: I Look Forward To:

Today's Self Love Activity: My Promise To Myself:

My Thoughts

In God, I Will Find The Strength I Need.

What Didn't Happen Will Not Become My Identity.

Peacefully Moving Forward

Date: Mood:

Today's Affirmation: I Am Learning:

I Am Intentionally Deciding: Today I Will Silence My Inner Critic By:

I Am Releasing: Today's Prayer:

Today I Have Hope That: I Look Forward To:

Today's Self Love Activity: My Promise To Myself:

My Thoughts

Peacefully Moving Forward

Date: Mood:

Today's Affirmation: I Am Learning:

I Am Intentionally Deciding: Today I Will Silence My Inner Critic By:

I Am Releasing: Today's Prayer:

Today I Have Hope That: I Look Forward To:

Today's Self Love Activity: My Promise To Myself:

My Thoughts

Peacefully Moving Forward

Date: Mood:

Today's Affirmation: I Am Learning:

I Am Intentionally Deciding: Today I Will Silence My Inner Critic By:

I Am Releasing: Today's Prayer:

Today I Have Hope That: I Look Forward To:

Today's Self Love Activity: My Promise To Myself:

My Thoughts

I Can And I Will Move Forward In Love.

You Are Deeply Loved.

Peacefully Moving Forward

Date: Mood:

Today's Affirmation: I Am Learning:

I Am Intentionally Deciding: Today I Will Silence My Inner Critic By:

I Am Releasing: Today's Prayer:

Today I Have Hope That: I Look Forward To:

Today's Self Love Activity: My Promise To Myself:

My Thoughts

Peacefully Moving Forward

Date: Mood:

Today's Affirmation: I Am Learning:

I Am Intentionally Deciding: Today I Will Silence My Inner Critic By:

I Am Releasing: Today's Prayer:

Today I Have Hope That: I Look Forward To:

Today's Self Love Activity: My Promise To Myself:

My Thoughts

I Feel Blessed....

I Trust My Journey And I Always Find My Way.

Peacefully Moving Forward

Date: Mood:

Today's Affirmation: I Am Learning:

I Am Intentionally Deciding: Today I Will Silence My Inner Critic By:

I Am Releasing: Today's Prayer:

Today I Have Hope That: I Look Forward To:

Today's Self Love Activity: My Promise To Myself:

My Thoughts

Peacefully Moving Forward

Date: Mood:

Today's Affirmation: I Am Learning:

I Am Intentionally Deciding: Today I Will Silence My Inner Critic By:

I Am Releasing: Today's Prayer:

Today I Have Hope That: I Look Forward To:

Today's Self Love Activity: My Promise To Myself:

My Thoughts

My Future Holds Tons Of Love And Happiness.

I Know Things Are Working In My Favor.

I Know I Am Not....

I Know I Am....

Peacefully Moving Forward

Date: Mood:

Today's Affirmation: I Am Learning:

I Am Intentionally Deciding: Today I Will Silence My Inner Critic By:

I Am Releasing: Today's Prayer:

Today I Have Hope That: I Look Forward To:

Today's Self Love Activity: My Promise To Myself:

My Thoughts

Peacefully Moving Forward

Date: Mood:

Today's Affirmation: I Am Learning:

I Am Intentionally Deciding: Today I Will Silence My Inner Critic By:

I Am Releasing: Today's Prayer:

Today I Have Hope That: I Look Forward To:

Today's Self Love Activity: My Promise To Myself:

My Thoughts

Peacefully Moving Forward

Date: Mood:

Today's Affirmation: I Am Learning:

I Am Intentionally Deciding: Today I Will Silence My Inner Critic By:

I Am Releasing: Today's Prayer:

Today I Have Hope That: I Look Forward To:

Today's Self Love Activity: My Promise To Myself:

My Thoughts

Peacefully Moving Forward

Date: Mood:

Today's Affirmation: I Am Learning:

I Am Intentionally Deciding: Today I Will Silence My Inner Critic By:

I Am Releasing: Today's Prayer:

Today I Have Hope That: I Look Forward To:

Today's Self Love Activity: My Promise To Myself:

My Thoughts

Peacefully Moving Forward

Date: Mood:

Today's Affirmation: I Am Learning:

I Am Intentionally Deciding: Today I Will Silence My Inner Critic By:

I Am Releasing: Today's Prayer:

Today I Have Hope That: I Look Forward To:

Today's Self Love Activity: My Promise To Myself:

My Thoughts

God Is Bringing Me To The Place He Wants Me To Be.

I Strongly Believe....

Peacefully Moving Forward

Date: Mood:

Today's Affirmation: I Am Learning:

I Am Intentionally Deciding: Today I Will Silence My Inner Critic By:

I Am Releasing: Today's Prayer:

Today I Have Hope That: I Look Forward To:

Today's Self Love Activity: My Promise To Myself:

My Thoughts

Peacefully Moving Forward

Date: Mood:

Today's Affirmation: I Am Learning:

I Am Intentionally Deciding: Today I Will Silence My Inner Critic By:

I Am Releasing: Today's Prayer:

Today I Have Hope That: I Look Forward To:

Today's Self Love Activity: My Promise To Myself:

My Thoughts

Peacefully Moving Forward

Date: Mood:

Today's Affirmation: I Am Learning:

I Am Intentionally Deciding: Today I Will Silence My Inner Critic By:

I Am Releasing: Today's Prayer:

Today I Have Hope That: I Look Forward To:

Today's Self Love Activity: My Promise To Myself:

My Thoughts

I Know I Am To Be A Mother Because....

The Experience Of Carrying My Baby Felt....

Peacefully Moving Forward

Date: Mood:

Today's Affirmation: I Am Learning:

I Am Intentionally Deciding: Today I Will Silence My Inner Critic By:

I Am Releasing: Today's Prayer:

Today I Have Hope That: I Look Forward To:

Today's Self Love Activity: My Promise To Myself:

My Thoughts

Peacefully Moving Forward

Date: Mood:

Today's Affirmation: I Am Learning:

I Am Intentionally Deciding: Today I Will Silence My Inner Critic By:

I Am Releasing: Today's Prayer:

Today I Have Hope That: I Look Forward To:

Today's Self Love Activity: My Promise To Myself:

My Thoughts

Peacefully Moving Forward

Date: Mood:

Today's Affirmation: I Am Learning:

I Am Intentionally Deciding: Today I Will Silence My Inner Critic By:

I Am Releasing: Today's Prayer:

Today I Have Hope That: I Look Forward To:

Today's Self Love Activity: My Promise To Myself:

My Thoughts

I Am Okay.

My Heart Felt....

Now My Heart Feels....

I Love My Beautiful And Powerful Female Body.

Peacefully Moving Forward

Date: Mood:

Today's Affirmation: I Am Learning:

I Am Intentionally Deciding: Today I Will Silence My Inner Critic By:

I Am Releasing: Today's Prayer:

Today I Have Hope That: I Look Forward To:

Today's Self Love Activity: My Promise To Myself:

My Thoughts

Peacefully Moving Forward

Date: Mood:

Today's Affirmation: I Am Learning:

I Am Intentionally Deciding: Today I Will Silence My Inner Critic By:

I Am Releasing: Today's Prayer:

Today I Have Hope That: I Look Forward To:

Today's Self Love Activity: My Promise To Myself:

My Thoughts

My Baby Has Siblings That Are Coming.

I Still Believe....

Peacefully Moving Forward

Date: Mood:

Today's Affirmation: I Am Learning:

I Am Intentionally Deciding: Today I Will Silence My Inner Critic By:

I Am Releasing: Today's Prayer:

Today I Have Hope That: I Look Forward To:

Today's Self Love Activity: My Promise To Myself:

My Thoughts

Peacefully Moving Forward

Date: Mood:

Today's Affirmation: I Am Learning:

I Am Intentionally Deciding: Today I Will Silence My Inner Critic By:

I Am Releasing: Today's Prayer:

Today I Have Hope That: I Look Forward To:

Today's Self Love Activity: My Promise To Myself:

My Thoughts

This Experience Has....

My Dreams Will Still Come True.

Peacefully Moving Forward

Date: Mood:

Today's Affirmation: I Am Learning:

I Am Intentionally Deciding: Today I Will Silence My Inner Critic By:

I Am Releasing: Today's Prayer:

Today I Have Hope That: I Look Forward To:

Today's Self Love Activity: My Promise To Myself:

My Thoughts

Peacefully Moving Forward

Date: Mood:

Today's Affirmation: I Am Learning:

I Am Intentionally Deciding: Today I Will Silence My Inner Critic By:

I Am Releasing: Today's Prayer:

Today I Have Hope That: I Look Forward To:

Today's Self Love Activity: My Promise To Myself:

My Thoughts

Peacefully Moving Forward

Date: Mood:

Today's Affirmation: I Am Learning:

I Am Intentionally Deciding: Today I Will Silence My Inner Critic By:

I Am Releasing: Today's Prayer:

Today I Have Hope That: I Look Forward To:

Today's Self Love Activity: My Promise To Myself:

My Thoughts

Peacefully Moving Forward

Date: Mood:

Today's Affirmation: I Am Learning:

I Am Intentionally Deciding: Today I Will Silence My Inner Critic By:

I Am Releasing: Today's Prayer:

Today I Have Hope That: I Look Forward To:

Today's Self Love Activity: My Promise To Myself:

My Thoughts

I Envision Myself....

I Was Made To Keep Going Even When It's Hard.

Peacefully Moving Forward

Date: Mood:

Today's Affirmation: I Am Learning:

I Am Intentionally Deciding: Today I Will Silence My Inner Critic By:

I Am Releasing: Today's Prayer:

Today I Have Hope That: I Look Forward To:

Today's Self Love Activity: My Promise To Myself:

My Thoughts

Because Of What Happened, I Now....

No Longer Will I Be Afraid.

Peacefully Moving Forward

Date: Mood:

Today's Affirmation: I Am Learning:

I Am Intentionally Deciding: Today I Will Silence My Inner Critic By:

I Am Releasing: Today's Prayer:

Today I Have Hope That: I Look Forward To:

Today's Self Love Activity: My Promise To Myself:

My Thoughts

Peacefully Moving Forward

Date: Mood:

Today's Affirmation: I Am Learning:

I Am Intentionally Deciding: Today I Will Silence My Inner Critic By:

I Am Releasing: Today's Prayer:

Today I Have Hope That: I Look Forward To:

Today's Self Love Activity: My Promise To Myself:

My Thoughts

Peacefully Moving Forward

Date: Mood:

Today's Affirmation: I Am Learning:

I Am Intentionally Deciding: Today I Will Silence My Inner Critic By:

I Am Releasing: Today's Prayer:

Today I Have Hope That: I Look Forward To:

Today's Self Love Activity: My Promise To Myself:

My Thoughts

I Find Myself....

God Will Use Me To Tell An Amazing Story.

Peacefully Moving Forward

Date: Mood:

Today's Affirmation: I Am Learning:

I Am Intentionally Deciding: Today I Will Silence My Inner Critic By:

I Am Releasing: Today's Prayer:

Today I Have Hope That: I Look Forward To:

Today's Self Love Activity: My Promise To Myself:

My Thoughts

Peacefully Moving Forward

Date: Mood:

Today's Affirmation: I Am Learning:

I Am Intentionally Deciding: Today I Will Silence My Inner Critic By:

I Am Releasing: Today's Prayer:

Today I Have Hope That: I Look Forward To:

Today's Self Love Activity: My Promise To Myself:

My Thoughts

Peacefully Moving Forward

Date: Mood:

Today's Affirmation: | I Am Learning:

I Am Intentionally Deciding: | Today I Will Silence My Inner Critic By:

I Am Releasing: | Today's Prayer:

Today I Have Hope That: | I Look Forward To:

Today's Self Love Activity: | My Promise To Myself:

My Thoughts

I Trust God.

You Are My Sunshine And I Will Keep Shining Knowing You Were Glowing Within Me.

Peacefully Moving Forward

Date: Mood:

Today's Affirmation: I Am Learning:

I Am Intentionally Deciding: Today I Will Silence My Inner Critic By:

I Am Releasing: Today's Prayer:

Today I Have Hope That: I Look Forward To:

Today's Self Love Activity: My Promise To Myself:

My Thoughts

Peacefully Moving Forward

Date: Mood:

Today's Affirmation: I Am Learning:

I Am Intentionally Deciding: Today I Will Silence My Inner Critic By:

I Am Releasing: Today's Prayer:

Today I Have Hope That: I Look Forward To:

Today's Self Love Activity: My Promise To Myself:

My Thoughts

Peacefully Moving Forward

Date: Mood:

Today's Affirmation: I Am Learning:

I Am Intentionally Deciding: Today I Will Silence My Inner Critic By:

I Am Releasing: Today's Prayer:

Today I Have Hope That: I Look Forward To:

Today's Self Love Activity: My Promise To Myself:

My Thoughts

I
Love
You.

You Will Always Be Family.

Peacefully Moving Forward

Date: Mood:

Today's Affirmation: I Am Learning:

I Am Intentionally Deciding: Today I Will Silence My Inner Critic By:

I Am Releasing: Today's Prayer:

Today I Have Hope That: I Look Forward To:

Today's Self Love Activity: My Promise To Myself:

My Thoughts

Peacefully Moving Forward

Date: Mood:

Today's Affirmation: I Am Learning:

I Am Intentionally Deciding: Today I Will Silence My Inner Critic By:

I Am Releasing: Today's Prayer:

Today I Have Hope That: I Look Forward To:

Today's Self Love Activity: My Promise To Myself:

My Thoughts

Made in the USA
Columbia, SC
16 June 2019